Texas Cowboys

by Linda B. Ross

Table of Contents

Introduction

What picture comes to mind when you hear the word *cowboy*? Do you see a man riding tall in the saddle? Does he wear a cowboy hat? What other details do you see?

The Texas cowboy has become an American folk hero. He has been celebrated in books, songs, and movies.

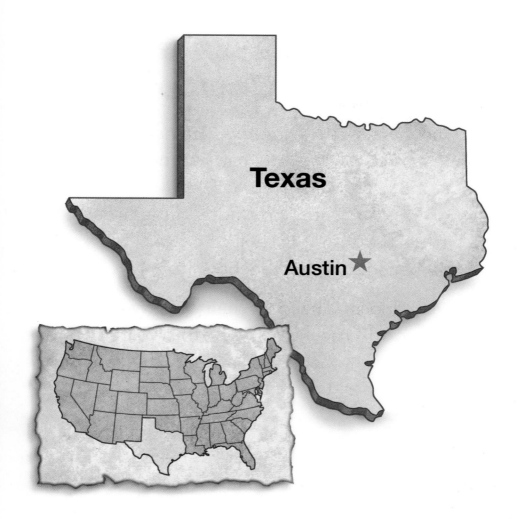

When people think about Texas, they often think about cowboys. Why do they connect the two? Cowboys played a major role in the history of Texas. They are still a big part of Texas life today.

CHAPTER 1

Early Cowboys

The first settlers in Texas came from Spain and Mexico. They were cattle ranchers. In fact, the word *ranch* comes from the Spanish word, *rancho*. Later on, more settlers came from all parts of the United States. Many of them became cattle ranchers, too.

The ranchers needed men to **drive** their cattle north. They could sell their cattle for a good price in the Northeast. So the ranchers hired cowboys to do the job.

The Price of Cattle

In the 1860s, a head of cattle could be sold for about $5 in Texas.

However, in the North, the same animal could be sold for $40.

A cattle drive that began in Texas might end up in places such as Kansas or Missouri. From there, railroads took the cattle to the Northeast.

A cattle drive could take several months. During that time, cowboys had to deal with all kinds of weather and often runaway cattle.

Driving **longhorn** cattle was hard work. Longhorns were a wild breed, and often they ran off. A **stampede** caused quite a commotion!

Cowboys put up with other hardships, as well. Sometimes the weather was bitter cold. Cowboys were shivering as they worked. Sometimes there were rivers to cross. That wasn't easy with a large herd of cattle! But nothing stopped the cowboys or rattled them. They had a job to do.

Stampedes

Stampedes often happened at night. The sound of thunder or a flash of lightning could cause a stampede. Once a stampede started, it might take hours for a group of cowboys to round up the cattle again. It was also very dangerous. If a cowboy's horse tripped and fell, the cowboy and his horse got trampled by the stampeding cattle.

CHAPTER 2

Famous Cowboys

Most cowboys didn't try to become famous. But some achieved fame anyway. In 1866, Charles Goodnight and Oliver Loving started out with 2,000 cattle and 18 cowboys. They wanted to drive the cattle from Texas to Colorado.

Goodnight was the scout for the drive. He rode ahead to make sure there would be enough grass and water for the cattle. Loving stayed behind to manage the herd. They made a good team!

Charles Goodnight

Oliver Loving

Charles Goodnight and Oliver Loving were pioneers. They were among the first people to help the cattle industry grow in Texas.

Goodnight and Loving traveled west and then north to Denver, Colorado. The Goodnight-Loving Trail was named in their honor.

Goodnight and Loving carved out a new route to the West. Their route was known as the Goodnight-Loving Trail. It became a popular route for driving cattle to Colorado and Wyoming. The Goodnight-Loving Trail opened up the **frontier** for many other cattle drivers.

Goodnight and Loving

Oliver Loving died in 1867, only a year after he and Charles Goodnight went on their famous drive. Charles Goodnight lived until 1929. He became a wealthy cattle rancher. He crossed longhorn cattle with Hereford cattle to create a new breed.

7

In 1997, Bose Ikard was honored by the Texas Trail of Fame. There is also a statue of him at the Stockyards in Fort Worth, Texas.

Bose Ikard was born a slave in Mississippi. In 1852, he came to Texas and later became a cowboy. Ikard was one of the cowboys on the Goodnight-Loving Trail drive. He helped fight off **bandits** who attacked the drivers and the herd.

Ikard worked with Charles Goodnight for many years. The two men formed a close friendship. They trusted and respected each other. Bose Ikard died in 1929. He is buried in the same cemetery in Weatherford, Texas, as his friend, Charles Goodnight.

John Baker Omohundro was born in 1846. His nickname was "Texas Jack." He worked as a scout and trail guide for the U.S. Cavalry. Later on, he starred in "The Scouts of the Prairie" stage shows with Buffalo Bill Cody.

Texas Jack was also a writer. He wrote about his life as a cowboy for a New York newspaper. Texas Jack was very young when he died in 1880. But he lived a very full life.

Texas Jack was a man of many talents.

Bill Pickett was the first African American to be honored by the Rodeo Hall of Fame. He was also honored by the Museum of the American Cowboy.

William "Bill" Pickett learned his cowboy skills at a young age. Later on, he became a famous **rodeo** star. Pickett wasn't afraid to tangle with any steer. In fact, he invented the rodeo event called steer wrestling.

Pickett performed with the Miller Brothers' 101 Ranch Wild West Show. This was one of the best shows that featured rodeo events. Pickett was a great performer. He amazed audiences all over the United States.

CHAPTER 3

Cowboys Today

Some people think cowboys have an easier life today than the cowboys of long ago. Why? Cowboys today don't have to go on long cattle drives. Ranches are fenced in and cattle are contained. Many cowboys ride in trucks or jeeps to herd cattle. Cowboys that work on large ranches even use helicopters!

Today's cowboys don't sleep outdoors or in drafty barns, either. They live in pleasant, modern rooms. After work, they can watch TV or drive to town. Cowboy life is not as hard or lonely as it used to be.

This "helicopter cowboy" is keeping track of cattle on a very large ranch.

New technology, such as the cell phone, has made a big difference in the life of a cowboy.

Most cowboys have cell phones today. Cell phones help them stay in touch with the rancher. If they need his or her advice, they can call. If there is a problem, they can get help quickly.

Back in the days of cattle drives, cowboys were on their own. There were no phones, and the rancher was many miles away. So it was up to the cowboy to solve any problems.

But in other ways, the lives of cowboys haven't changed so much. They still wake up at dawn to begin their day's work. They still work until the sun goes down. Many cowboys who use trucks and jeeps also ride horses to herd cattle. Cowboys still spend a great amount of time outdoors.

Clothing	Purpose
cowboy hat	It protects the cowboy from the weather: sun, rain, and cold.
bandana	It protects the cowboy's neck from the sun. It can also be used as a dust mask.
chaps	They protect the cowboy's legs from shrubs and cactus.
boots	They protect the cowboy's feet and lower legs. The heels on the boots help him keep his feet in the stirrups when he rides his horse.

cowboy hat

bandana

chaps

boots

Many cowboys wear the same kinds of outfits as the cowboys of yesterday.

Conclusion

There may be fewer cowboys today than in the past. But cowboys are still an important part of Texas life.

The cattle industry depends on cowboys. Cattle ranches could not run without cowboys. Cowboys also perform in rodeos and keep the rodeo tradition alive. It is no wonder that cowboys were heroes of the past, and that they are still heroes today.

Glossary

bandits (*BAN-dits*) robbers or criminals *(page 8)*

drive (*DRIGHV*) to move a herd of cattle from one place to a distant place *(page 4)*

frontier (*frun-TEER*) part of the country that hasn't been settled *(page 7)*

longhorn (*LAWNG-hawrn*) a breed of cattle that has very long horns *(page 5)*

rodeo (*ROH-dee-oh*) contest or show of skill in roping cattle or riding horses and steers *(page 10)*

stampede (*stam-PEED*) herd of cattle running wild *(page 5)*

Index

Comprehension Check

Retell

Use a Cause and Effect Chart and the photos to help you retell what you learned in this book.

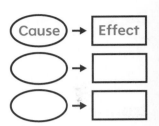

Think and Compare

1. Turn to page 4. What was the reason ranchers hired cowboys long ago? *(Cause and Effect)*

2. What do you believe is the best thing about being a cowboy? *(Apply)*

3. In what way might a cowboy's life be different in the future? *(Analyze)*